Essential COOKING SERIES

COMPREHENSIVE, STEP BY STEP COOKING

Salads & Greens

HINKLER
BOOKS

Food Editor:Ellen Argyriou
Project Editor: Lara Morcombe
Design: Studio Pazzo
Cover design: Hinkler Books Studio

Essential Cooking Series: Salads & Greens
First published in 2005 by Hinkler Books Pty Ltd
45-55 Fairchild Street
Heatherton, Victoria 3202 Australia
www.hinklerbooks.com

ISBN-13: 978-1-7412-1943-2

Printed and bound in China

10 9 8 7 6
10 09 08 07

Contents

An introduction to salads and greens

Crisp, refreshing, colourful, delicious, light, appealing, wholesome and healthy are all the words which come to mind when we think of salads. They are nature's gift to our health status and to our meal table.

The value of salads in our diet cannot be underestimated. They provide, first and foremost, valuable nutrients such as vitamins and minerals, which are not lost through cooking. They add variety and interest to our diet, colour to our table and elevate the most simple meal.

Salad ingredients were once restricted to the traditional varieties of the various cuisines around the world. Today, with the interchange of ethnic cuisines the demand for new salad produce has crossed continents and climatic zones and everything is available to all. We can all enjoy salad combinations outside our own traditional fare. We can combine the fruits of the tropics with the vegetables of the temperate zones, the flavours of the west with the more exotic flavours of the east. This book explores this amazing interchange.

Salads are not only for summer meals, they can and should be served all the year.

The following salad greens are known by several names. This guide will assist you to identify the ingredient you require.

Cos lettuce
Has a crisp leaf and a sweetish nutty flavour. Known as: cos, romaine.

Iceberg lettuce
Crisp leaves packed tightly into a round head. Known as: iceberg lettuce, crisphead lettuce.

Mignonette lettuce
Soft tender leaves tinged with red. Known as: mignonette lettuce, cabbage lettuce.

Green and red coral lettuce
Green or red frilled leaves. Do not form a heart. Known as: green coral or red coral, loose-leaf lettuce.

Butter lettuce
Tender soft leaf lettuce with buttery flavour. Known as: butter lettuce, butterhead.

Endive
Crisp leaf with a slight bitter flavour. Known as: endive, chicory, curly endive.

Rocket
A flavoursome leaf with a mustard tang. Known as: rocket, roquette, arugula.

Radicchio
A beautiful ruby colour with thick white veins; a very attractive leaf for presentation. Known as: radicchio, red leaved chicory, Italian chicory, Italian red lettuce.

Witlof
Crisp white leaves with a sharp mild bitter flavour. Known as: witlof, Belgian endive, French endive, witlof chicory.

Spring onions
A young bulb onion harvested before the bulb has formed. With a mild flavour and crisp texture, it is in great demand for salads. Known as: fresh green onions, spring onions, scallions, Welsh onions, bunching onions.

Spanish onions
Red in colour, these onions have a mild sweetish flavour. There are many varieties. Known as: Spanish onion, Italian red onion.

Flat-leaf parsley
Parsley with a flat leaf and a more intense flavour than the curly parsley. Known as: flat-leaf parsley, continental parsley.

Salad tips and skills

Salad greens and other salad vegetables must be stored correctly to retain freshness and quality. Do not wash any vegetables before storing. Greens that are tied in bunches such as spinach, endive and rocket should be opened out and checked. If damp in the centre, pat dry before storing.

Salad greens should be stored in the vegetable compartment of the refrigerator. As the level of vegetables in the compartment lowers, place a clean kitchen towel lightly over their surface to prevent moisture being drawn from them to fill the space. Have you ever wondered why the last few pieces in the vegetable compartment have wilted?

If there is no room in the vegetable container, salad vegetables may be placed on the lower shelves in a plastic bag, covered plastic container or on a tray covered with a clean cloth or plastic wrap. The important point is to cover their surface to prevent moisture loss.

Root vegetables may be stored on a rack in a well-ventilated dark place. All vegetables and fruits must be washed well before peeling and cutting.

Salad greens must be washed well in 2–3 changes of water to remove all grit, or in a colander under trickling cold water, not to bruise the tender leaves. Drain well.

Root vegetables need to be scrubbed with a brush under running water to remove all dirt, particularly if being cooked with the skin on.

For a good salad, leaves need to be dried well before placing in the bowl. The dressing will not adhere to wet leaves and the excess moisture will dilute the dressing. A salad spinner is excellent. It will spin all the water off. You may pat dry the leaves with absorbent paper or shake dry in a clean kitchen cloth.

To crisp the salad leaves roll up in a damp cloth and refrigerate for 1 hour or until you are ready to serve.

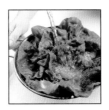 

Deseeding tomatoes

Cut the tomato in half across the centre. Cup the tomato in your hand and squeeze out the seeds.

To trim asparagus

Using a potato peeler or sharp paring knife peel off the thicker skin on the lower part of the stalk.

To segment an orange or grapefruit

1 Peel the orange or grapefruit thickly, removing all the white pith.

2 Holding the orange or grapefruit over a bowl to catch the juice, cut close to the membrane on each side of the segment and ease the segment out. Continue to the next segment.

To deseed a cucumber

Cut the cucumber in half lengthwise. Run the point of a teaspoon down the seeds, pressing inwards to remove the seeds.

To toast nuts

1 Place nuts on a shallow oven tray and place in a moderate oven 180°C (350°F, gas mark 4) for 10 minutes or until golden. The nuts will crisp on cooling. A deep colouration will impart a bitter flavour.

2 Heat a heavy-based frying pan until hot. Add the nuts and stir with a wooden spoon until they colour. Remove from the pan as soon as desired colour is attained.

To blanch almonds

Place in a bowl and cover with hot water. Stand for 10 minutes then slip off skins.

To peel capsicum

Trim the top and base of each capsicum and cut into quarters making 4 flat pieces. Trim off any inside veins and rub skin side with oil. Place skin side up, under a preheated hot grill and cook until skins are blistered. Place in a plastic bag closing the end and set aside until cool enough to handle. With the aid of a small knife lift the edge of the skin and peel off.

Favourite caesar salad

INGREDIENTS

5 cloves garlic, crushed
4 tablespoons olive oil
9 slices anchovies
juice of 1½ lemons
2 teaspoons worcestershire
  sauce
1 teaspoon mustard
1½ tablepoons white-wine
  vinegar
4 eggs
2 thick slices country-style bread
2 tablespoons olive oil
100 g (3½ oz) prosciutto
3 heads cos lettuce,
  washed and crisped
50 g (1¾ oz) parmesan
salt
freshly ground black pepper
serves 6–8

1 Preheat the oven to 220°C (430°F, gas mark 7). Cut the bread into cubes and toss with the olive oil and salt and pepper. Transfer to a baking tray and bake the cubes for 15 minutes until golden and cool. Crisp the prosciutto on a shallow tray in the oven for 3 minutes.

2 In a large mixing bowl, place garlic and olive oil, using the back of a metal spoon, press the garlic into the oil. Add the anchovies and mash into the oil mixture. Whisk in lemon juice, worcestershire sauce, mustard and white-wine vinegar, mixing each ingredient thoroughly before the next is added.

3 Boil the eggs for 1 minute. Remove immediately and allow to cool. Crack the egg carefully, separate the yolks and mix well into the ingredients in the bowl.

4 Place lettuce leaves in a mixing bowl and toss thoroughly in the dressing for several minutes until all leaves are coated. Add bread cubes, parmesan, and finish with black pepper and crisp prosciutto. Serve immediately.

PREPARATION TIME
15 minutes

COOKING TIME
15 minutes

NUTRITIONAL VALUE PER SERVE   FAT 9.5 G   CARBOHYDRATE 2.8 G   PROTEIN 5.1 G

Watercress and pear salad

INGREDIENTS

2 bunches watercress, plucked
and washed
3 tablespoons olive oil
1 tablespoon lemon juice
$\frac{1}{2}$ tablespoon white-wine vinegar
salt and pepper
3 beurre bosc pears, washed
parmesan shavings
serves 6–8

1 Slice pears finely and combine with watercress in a bowl.

2 Whisk oil, lemon juice and white-wine vinegar with salt and pepper until slightly thickened. Drizzle over salad just enough to coat the leaves. Place on a platter and top with shavings of parmesan.

PREPARATION TIME
8 minutes

| NUTRITIONAL VALUE PER SERVE | FAT 5.6 G | CARBOHYDRATE 6.4 G | PROTEIN 2.1 G |

Witlof salad with pecans

INGREDIENTS

5 heads witlof (Belgian endive),
  washed
1 red delicious apple, quartered
1 granny smith apple, quartered
juice of 1 lemon
200 g (7 oz) young rocket leaves
160 g (5½ oz) pecan nuts, coarsely
  chopped and toasted
100 g (3½ oz) gorgonzola or
  blue castello, crumbled
dressing
4 tablespoons olive oil
4 tablespoons walnut oil
4 tablespoons sherry-wine vinegar
1 large spring onion (green onion),
  finely chopped
salt and pepper
serves 6

1 Cut the witlof in half, lengthwise then lay the witlof cut side down on a board and cut the leaves into thin strips.

2 Toss apples with the lemon juice. Wash the rocket leaves and drain well.

3 In a bowl, combine witlof, apple slices, rocket, toasted pecans and blue cheese. Whisk together walnut and olive oil, sherry-wine vinegar and spring onion, and salt and pepper to taste. Drizzle over the salad and toss. Serve immediately.

PREPARATION TIME
15 minutes

NUTRITIONAL VALUE PER SERVE	FAT 8.2 G	CARBOHYDRATE 1.9 G	PROTEIN 2.3 G

King prawns with mango salsa

INGREDIENTS

12 raw king prawns, peeled (tails on)
seasoned flour for dusting
1 egg, beaten
155 g (5 oz) sesame seeds
90 g (3 oz) shredded coconut
1 mango, peeled and finely diced
½ small spanish onion, finely diced
2 tablespoons chopped coriander
juice of 1 lime
2 tablespoons butter or olive oil
150 g (5 oz) mixed salad greens
   of your choice
lime quarters for garnish
serves 4

PREPARATION TIME
15 minutes, plus 20
minutes refrigeration

COOKING TIME
3 minutes

1 Butterfly the prawns, cutting along the inner curve, ¾ of the way through and to the vein. Open out, remove the vein and flatten by pressing down with side of a large knife.

2 Dip each prawn into the seasoned flour then into the beaten egg to coat both sides. Place onto the coconut mixture, covering the top also, and pressing down lightly for the mixture to adhere. Place the prawns on a flat oven tray and refrigerate 20 minutes or more.

3 In a frying pan, heat the butter or olive oil, add prawns and fry over a high heat for 1–2 minutes each side until golden. (You may need to apply pressure with a spatula as they cook to prevent them from curling up.)

4 Combine mango, onion, coriander and lime juice in a bowl and season to taste. To serve, arrange some salad greens on each plate and top with 3 cooked prawns and a generous spoonful of the mango salsa. Drizzle over any remaining salsa juice and serve immediately with lime wedges if desired.

NUTRITIONAL VALUE PER SERVE	FAT 17.3 G	CARBOHYDRATE 3.7 G	PROTEIN 9.4 G

Rock lobster and smoked ocean trout salad

INGREDIENTS

2 lobster tails, cooked
400 g (13 oz) smoked ocean trout
1 continental cucumber
1 carrot
1 green zucchini (courgette)
1 yellow zucchini
100 g (3½ oz) rocket leaves
1 bunch chives, snipped
dressing
juice of 2 limes
1 tablespoon palm sugar
  or brown sugar
½ cup (125 ml, 4 fl oz) olive oil
salt and pepper
serves 6

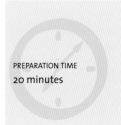

PREPARATION TIME
20 minutes

1 Remove the meat from the lobster tails and slice finely. Cut trout into thin strips. Place lobster and trout in a container, cover and refrigerate.

2 Wash the cucumber, slice in half lengthways, scoop out and discard the seeds. Using a potato peeler or vegetable slicer, cut the cucumber and carrot into long thin ribbons. Cut the unpeeled green and yellow zucchini into long thin ribbons. Mix the lobster, ocean trout, ribboned vegetables and rocket leaves gently together in a large bowl.

3 In a bowl, place the lime juice and palm sugar. Heat in the microwave or over hot water to dissolve the sugar. Whisk in the olive oil, add the salt and pepper and whisk until it thickens. Toss gently through the salad. Arrange the salad on an attractive platter and sprinkle over chives.

NUTRITIONAL VALUE PER SERVE	FAT 9.8 G	CARBOHYDRATE 1.9 G	PROTEIN 11 G

Armenian stuffed tomato salad

INGREDIENTS

8 large, round tomatoes
4 tablespoons olive oil
1 large onion, finely chopped
1 large leek, finely chopped
3 cups (555 g, 1 lb) steamed or
    boiled white or brown rice
80 g (2³/₄ oz) pine nuts, toasted
110 g (3¹/₂ oz) currants
1 handful parsley, chopped
1 tablespoon chopped fresh mint
³/₄ teaspoon sea salt
¹/₂ teaspoon black pepper
2 cloves garlic, peeled and smashed
¹/₂ cup (125 ml, 4 fl oz) vegetable stock
¹/₂ cup (125 ml, 4 fl oz) white wine
500 g (1 lb) baby spinach leaves,
    washed and drained
serves 8

1 Preheat the oven to 180°C (350°F, gas mark 4). With a sharp knife, slice the tops off the tomatoes, scoop out as much flesh as possible without damaging the exterior of the tomato. Chop the removed flesh finely.

2 Heat the oil in a frying pan and cook onion and leek until slightly golden. Add rice, tomato pulp, nuts, currants, parsley, mint, salt and pepper and sauté until the mixture is hot and well flavoured.

3 Fill each tomato with the rice mixture and replace the tops of the tomatoes. Place in a baking dish. Combine garlic, stock and white wine and pour around tomatoes. Bake for 20 minutes. Remove from oven.

4 Place spinach leaves in a bowl. Spoon some of the hot cooking liquid from the tomatoes over the spinach, discard the garlic, and toss well. Serve a mound of warm spinach on each plate with the tomato placed on top. Drizzle any remaining liquid over and serve.

PREPARATION TIME
20 minutes

COOKING TIME
20 minutes

NUTRITIONAL VALUE PER SERVE   FAT 4.3 G   CARBOHYDRATE 8.1 G   PROTEIN 1.8 G

Grilled goat's cheese salad

INGREDIENTS

4 small pieces of goat's cheese
2 sprigs fresh thyme
1 clove garlic, crushed
$^1/_3$ cup (80 ml, $2^3/_4$ fl oz)
    extra virgin olive oil
cracked black pepper
4 thin lemon slices, halved
300 g (10 oz) mixed salad leaves,
    washed and crisped
slices of country-style bread, toasted
serves 4

PREPARATION TIME
10 minutes

MARINATING TIME
4-6 hours

1 Place the cheese in a container which will fit tightly. Strip the thyme leaves from
   the stalk into a bowl. Add garlic, oil and cracked pepper and mix well. Pour over
   the cheese and place lemon slices between the cheese. Cover and marinate in
   the refrigerator for 4–6 hours. Turn cheese in the marinade once or twice.

2 Preheat the grill. Grill the cheese for 2 minutes each side and the lemon slices
   until rosy tinged and softened a little.

3 Arrange salad leaves on 4 plates. Place a piece of cheese and lemon slice on
   each and drizzle with marinade. Toast the bread and serve with the salad.

NUTRITIONAL VALUE PER SERVE   FAT 18.3 G   CARBOHYDRATE 1.1 G   PROTEIN 3.5 G

Warm lima bean and prosciutto salad with rocket

INGREDIENTS

420 g (14 oz) can lima beans
2 tablespoons olive oil
$^1/_2$ teaspoon dried chilli flakes
3 cloves garlic, finely chopped
100 g (3$^1/_2$ oz) prosciutto,
  roughly chopped
juice of 1 lemon
10 basil leaves, torn
1 bunch of rocket leaves
salt and freshly ground black pepper
serves 6

PREPARATION TIME
15 minutes

COOKING TIME
5 minutes

1 Drain the canned beans in a strainer and rinse through with cold water.

2 Heat oil in a large frying pan. Add chilli flakes and garlic and sauté
   briefly until garlic is golden. Add prosciutto and for about 2 minutes stir
   over moderate heat until beginning to brown. Add lima beans and cook
   for 3 minutes, while tossing occasionally and adding lemon juice.
   Remove from heat.

3 Add basil leaves and rocket, and season with salt and pepper. Toss
   gently then transfer to a platter. Serve warm.

NUTRITIONAL VALUE PER SERVE	FAT 3 G	CARBOHYDRATE 6.2 G	PROTEIN 4.9 G

Couscous salad with seafood and fresh mint

INGREDIENTS

¹/₂ cup (125 ml, 4 fl oz) olive oil
2 tablespoons lemon juice
1 large clove garlic, finely chopped
1 teaspoon celery seed
¹/₄ teaspoon turmeric
¹/₄ teaspoon cumin
1²/₃ cups (410 ml, 13 fl oz)
   vegetable stock
500 g (1 lb) raw king prawns,
   peeled (tails on)
200 g (7 oz) small calamari
   (squid) rings
300 g (10 oz) couscous
3 tomatoes, finely diced
2 stalks celery, finely sliced
6 spring onions (green onions),
   chopped
20 fresh mint leaves, finely sliced
salt and pepper
serves 6

1 Whisk together oil, lemon juice, garlic and celery seed until thick then season with salt and pepper. Set aside to develop flavour. In a pan, bring stock to the boil and add turmeric and cumin. Add prawns and calamari and poach gently for 2 minutes until the prawns are orange. Remove seafood from stock with a slotted spoon.

2 In a large bowl, place the couscous and pour over hot stock. Stir well and cover. Allow to stand for about 10 minutes until water is absorbed.

3 Toss couscous with a fork to fluff then add seafood. Toss in the diced tomatoes, celery, spring onions and some of the shredded mint leaves.

4 Add the dressing and mix well then garnish with remaining mint leaves.

PREPARATION TIME
20 minutes

COOKING TIME
5 minutes

NUTRITIONAL VALUE PER SERVE	FAT 5.4 G	CARBOHYDRATE 2.1 G	PROTEIN 6.7 G

Tuscan tomato and bean salad

INGREDIENTS

12 sun-dried tomato halves
1 cup (250 ml, 8 fl oz) boiling water
$^1/_3$ cup (80 ml, 2 $^3/_4$ fl oz) rice vinegar
1 tablespoon olive oil
2 teaspoons honey
salt and pepper to taste
150 g (5 oz) baby rocket leaves
150 g (5 oz) watercress
8 roma tomatoes, diced
6 fresh spring onions
  (green onions), sliced
80 g (2$^3/_4$ oz) kalamata olives,
  stones removed
2 x 440 g (14 oz) cans cannellini beans,
  rinsed and drained
100 g (3$^1/_2$ oz) toasted walnuts, chopped
serves 4–6

PREPARATION TIME
15 minutes

1 Soak the sun dried tomatoes in the boiling water until water cools. Add the rice vinegar, oil, honey and purée in a food processor until smooth. Add salt and pepper to taste.

2 Pluck the watercress sprigs from the coarse stems, and thoroughly wash with the rocket. Drain well and shake dry in a clean towel. Place in a large mixing bowl and add the diced tomatoes, green onions, olives and cannellini beans.

3 Pour over the sun-dried tomato dressing and toss well to coat. Serve immediately garnished with the toasted walnuts.

NUTRITIONAL VALUE PER SERVE	FAT 3.4 G	CARBOHYDRATE 7.1 G	PROTEIN 3.9 G

Herbed seafood salad

INGREDIENTS

24 poached scallops
24 king prawns, peeled,
  de-veined and cooked
4 tablespoons vinegar
4 tablespoons lime juice
3 tablespoons orange juice
1 clove garlic, lightly crushed
1 red chilli, deseeded
  and finely sliced
¼ green capsicum (pepper),
  cut into fine strips
60 g (2 oz) stuffed green olives, halved
2 tablespoons chopped
  fresh coriander
½ cup (125 ml, 4 fl oz) light olive oil
lemon slices and dandelion
  leaves for serving
serves 8

PREPARATION TIME
**10 minutes, plus
2 hours refrigeration**

COOKING TIME
4 minutes

1 Place scallops in a saucepan with just enough hot water to cover. Bring to a slow simmer and simmer for 2 minutes. Allow to cool in the liquid. In a bowl, combine scallops and prawns. Add vinegar, lime and orange juice and garlic. Mix well, cover and chill for 2 hours.

2 Strain seafood mixture, reserving marinade. In a salad bowl, place seafood and add chilli, green capsicum, olives and coriander. Toss. Add oil to reserved marinade and whisk well. Pour dressing over salad and toss lightly. Place a few dandelion leaves on each plate. Pile the salad in the centre and garnish with lemon.

NUTRITIONAL VALUE PER SERVE   FAT 10.4 G   CARBOHYDRATE 0.7 G   PROTEIN 13.7 G

Summer salad of grilled chicken, spinach and mango

INGREDIENTS

salad

6 roma tomatoes
10 basil leaves, chopped
10 mint leaves, chopped
salt and black pepper
$^1/_2$ teaspoon sugar
12 chicken tenderloins (from breasts)
1 bunch of asparagus, trimmed
   and steamed
1 avocado, diced
1 bunch spring onions
   (green onions), diagonally sliced
8 firm button mushrooms, sliced
2 firm mangoes, peeled and
   cut into dice
150 g (5 oz) baby spinach leaves
60 g (2 oz) toasted hazelnuts,
   lightly crushed
60 g (2 oz) toasted brazil nuts,
   lightly crushed
60 g (2 oz) toasted pistachio nuts,
   lightly crushed

dressing

2 teaspoons honey
2 tablespoons balsamic vinegar
3 tablespoons raspberry vinegar
2 teaspoons dijon mustard
2 teaspoons finely chopped ginger
2 cloves garlic, crushed
2 tablespoons lemon juice
2 tablespoons olive oil
salt and freshly ground black pepper

serves 6

PREPARATION TIME
30 minutes, plus
2 hours refrigeration

COOKING TIME
2 hours

1 Preheat oven 160°C (315°F, gas mark 2–3). Slice the tomatoes in half lengthways, and top with basil, mint, salt, pepper and sugar. Bake for 2 hours. When cooked and cool, slice each half in two.

2 Whisk together honey, vinegars, dijon mustard, ginger, garlic, lemon juice, olive oil and salt and pepper until thick. Place chicken tenderloins in a container, pour over $^1/_2$ the dressing. Cover and allow to marinate for 2 hours or more in the refrigerator. Heat a non-stick grill pan and cook the chicken fillets over a high heat for 2–3 minutes on each side until cooked through. Transfer fillets to a plate and keep warm.

3 In a large bowl, place spinach leaves and add asparagus, spring onions, mushrooms and roasted tomatoes. Add remaining dressing and toss thoroughly.

4 Divide the salad evenly amongst individual plates and add some mango and avocado cubes. Top with 2 fillets of chicken, and a generous sprinkling of nuts. Serve immediately.

NUTRITIONAL VALUE PER SERVE	FAT 7.5 G	CARBOHYDRATE 3 G	PROTEIN 8 G

Ocean trout with palm sugar sauce and noodle salad

INGREDIENTS

2 tablespoons olive oil
10 spring onions (green onions),
  chopped
200 g (7 oz) palm sugar
100 ml (3½ fl oz) fish sauce
110 g (3½ oz) fresh ginger,
  cut into fine strips
10 small chillies, deseeded and
  cut into fine strips
2 tablespoons lime juice
200 g (7 oz) cellophane noodles
1 bunch fresh coriander, chopped
500 g (1 lb) ocean trout fillets,
  cut into 3 cm-wide pieces
extra coriander, for garnish
serves 4

PREPARATION TIME
15 minutes

COOKING TIME
10 minutes

1 Heat the oil in a small frying pan and gently sauté the spring onions until golden. Add the palm sugar and heat until dissolved. Cook on a medium heat for about 5 minutes until the mixture has caramelised, stir well. Add the fish sauce, ginger, chillies and lime juice. Stir well to combine. Remove from heat and cover.

2 Soak the cellophane noodles in hot water for about 10 minutes until softened, then refresh in cold water. Drain and place in a bowl. Add the coriander leaves and enough palm sugar sauce to moisten the noodles.

3 Pan fry or grill the fish fillets for about 2 minutes each side until just cooked. Arrange the cellophane noodle salad on individual plates then place the fish pieces on top. Garnish with coriander leaves and spoon over more sauce.

NUTRITIONAL VALUE PER SERVE	FAT 4.4 G	CARBOHYDRATE 18 G	PROTEIN 9.8 G

Tomato salad napolitano

INGREDIENTS

6 large ripe tomatoes,
  each cut into 8 wedges
1 Spanish onion, thinly sliced
185 g (6 oz) pecorino cheese,
  coarsely grated
2 teaspoons shredded fresh basil
1 teaspoon chopped fresh oregano
vinaigrette
⅓ cup (90 ml, 3 fl oz) olive oil
4 tablespoons white-wine vinegar
½ teaspoon sugar
½ teaspoon salt
¼ teaspoon pepper
serves 6

PREPARATION TIME
10 minutes

1 In a large bowl, combine tomato wedges and onion slices. Add the
   cheese and mix well.

2 In a small bowl, whisk together olive oil, white-wine vinegar,
   sugar, salt and pepper. In another bowl, place the basil and
   oregano. Mix in the vinaigrette. Pour over the tomato mixture and
   toss well. Serve at room temperature.

NUTRITIONAL VALUE PER SERVE	FAT 8.3 G	CARBOHYDRATE 1.9 G	PROTEIN 4.2 G

Calabrian salad

INGREDIENTS

4 medium potatoes, unpeeled
8 firm roma tomatoes
3 Spanish onions, sliced thinly
15 small basil leaves
1 heaped teaspoon dried oregano
4 tablespoons olive oil
3 tablespoons white-
   or red-wine vinegar
salt and pepper to taste
serves 6

PREPARATION TIME
15 minutes

COOKING TIME
20 minutes

1 Cover potatoes in cold water and boil for 15–20 minutes until just tender. Drain and leave aside until just cool enough to handle, then peel and slice thinly. Place Spanish onions in cold water and soak for 30 minutes. Drain.

2 Cut tomatoes in half and slice. In a bowl, combine potatoes, tomatoes and Spanish onion.

3 Add basil leaves, oregano, olive oil, vinegar and salt and pepper. Toss carefully and serve immediately.

NUTRITIONAL VALUE PER SERVE	FAT 3.8 G	CARBOHYDRATE 5.8 G	PROTEIN 1.5 G

Roasted beetroot, orange and fennel salad

INGREDIENTS

5 large beetroots
1 tablespoon brown sugar
1 teaspoon salt
2 tablespoons chopped
  fresh rosemary
3 tablespoons olive oil
1 bulb fennel
3 blood oranges, segmented
150 g (5 oz) hazelnuts,
  crushed and toasted
dressing
1 handful dill, chopped
2 tablespoons balsamic vinegar
½ cup (125 ml, 4 fl oz) olive oil
salt and pepper
serves 4–6

PREPARATION TIME
20 minutes

COOKING TIME
1 hour

1 Preheat the oven to 180°C (350°F, gas mark 4). Wash and trim the beetroots at root and stem ends leaving 1 cm of root and stem but do not peel. In a small bowl, combine brown sugar, 1 teaspoon salt, rosemary and 3 tablespoons olive oil until well-blended. Add whole beetroots and toss in oil mixture. Wrap each beetroot in foil and place in a baking dish. Roast for approximately 1 hour until just tender. Peel the beetroot by sliding off the skin with your fingers then cut into thick slices.

2 Trim tops and base of the fennel bulb and cut in half. Remove a wedge of tough core from each half making a 'v' cut at centre. Slice finely lengthwise.

3 Combine the dill, balsamic vinegar, remaining olive oil and salt and pepper to taste. Whisk well until thick. Arrange beetroots on a serving platter with the thinly sliced fennel and orange. Drizzle over the dill vinaigrette, then scatter the hazelnuts on top.

NUTRITIONAL VALUE PER SERVE	FAT 5.8 G	CARBOHYDRATE 7.8 G	PROTEIN 2.6 G

Kiwifruit and watercress salad

INGREDIENTS

½ bunch watercress, washed drained
and dried
3 kiwifruit
125 g (4 oz) small white button
mushrooms
75 g (2½ oz) drained sun-dried
tomatoes, packed in oil
dressing
2 tablespoons virgin olive oil
1 tablespoon red-wine vinegar
½ teaspoon salt
freshly ground black pepper
serves 4

PREPARATION TIME
15 minutes

1 Pluck the sprigs from the watercress discarding the coarse stems.
Peel and slice the kiwifruit. Place sprigs and kiwifruit into a large
bowl.

2 Wipe mushrooms over damp kitchen paper and trim the ends of
the stems. Slice thinly and add to the bowl. Cut the sun-dried
tomatoes in half, add to the bowl and toss lightly to distribute the
ingredients.

3 In a jug, whisk together oil, vinegar, salt and pepper. Drizzle over
the salad in a thin stream and toss gently. Divide between 4 salad
plates and serve immediately.

| NUTRITIONAL VALUE PER SERVE | FAT 7.9 G | CARBOHYDRATE 6.8 G | PROTEIN 2.4 G |

Spinach grapefruit salad

INGREDIENTS

1 bunch fresh young spinach leaves,
   rinsed and dried, leaves torn into
   pieces
1 large grapefruit, segmented
½ Spanish onion, diced
½ small red cabbage, shredded
3 tablespoons olive oil
2 tablespoons red-wine vinegar
3 tablespoons orange juice
salt and pepper to taste
rind (zest) of 1 orange, cut into strips
serves 4

PREPARATION TIME
10 minutes

1 In a salad bowl, place spinach, grapefruit, onion and cabbage. Toss well.

2 In a small bowl, whisk together oil, vinegar, orange juice and salt and
pepper. Pour over the salad and toss lightly. Serve at once, garnished
with thin strips of orange rind.

NUTRITIONAL VALUE PER SERVE	FAT 4.8 G	CARBOHYDRATE 3.0 G	PROTEIN 1.6 G

Marinated chicken and pear salad

INGREDIENTS

1 large cooked chicken, chopped
into 1 cm-wide strips
200 g (7 oz) dried pear halves,
halved again

salad

1 coral lettuce
1 mignonette lettuce
1 bunch rocket
2 Lebanese cucumbers, thinly sliced
1 small Spanish onion, thinly sliced
1 tablespoon olive oil

marinade

½ cup (125 ml, 4 fl oz) olive oil
½ cup (125 ml, 4 fl oz) orange juice
40 g (1¼ oz) seeded raisins
2 tablespoons red-wine vinegar
3 whole cloves
2 tablespoons pine nuts
½ teaspoon finely chopped red chilli
salt and pepper

serves 12

1 In a flat-based container, place chicken and top with pears.

2 In a bowl, combine orange juice, raisins, vinegar, cloves, pine nuts, red chilli, ½ cup olive oil, and salt and pepper to taste. Pour over the chicken. Cover and refrigerate at least 3 hours. Turn chicken and pears after 1½ hours so top pieces sit in the marinade. Wrap washed lettuce leaves and rocket in a damp cloth and refrigerate to crisp.

3 Place salad leaves on a platter and arrange over the chicken, pears, cucumber and onions. Spoon over pine nuts and raisins from the marinade. Whisk the remaining marinade again with the extra oil and drizzle over the salad.

PREPARATION TIME
25 minutes, plus
3 hours marinating

NUTRITIONAL VALUE PER SERVE   FAT 9.6 G   CARBOHYDRATE 7.1 G   PROTEIN 6.6 G

Pasta salad with snow peas and salami

INGREDIENTS

155 g (5 oz) pasta shells
185 g (6 oz) snow peas (mangetout), trimmed
125 g (4 oz) Italian salami, sliced and cut into matchsticks
1 carrot, cut into matchsticks
90 g (3 oz) mozzarella cheese, shredded
vinaigrette
4 tablespoons olive oil
2 tablespoons white-wine vinegar
¼ teaspoon sugar
¼ teaspoon salt
¼ teaspoon pepper
serves 4

1 Cook pasta shells in a pan of boiling water for about 12 minutes until al dente. Drain, rinse under cold running water and drain again.

2 Plunge snow peas into a pan of boiling water. Bring back to the boil and cook for 30 seconds. Drain immediately and plunge into a bowl of iced water for 2 minutes. Drain and pat dry with paper towels.

3 In a salad bowl, combine pasta shells, snow peas, salami, carrot and mozzarella. In a small bowl, combine olive oil, white-wine vinegar, sugar, salt and pepper. Drizzle vinaigrette over pasta and toss well. Serve lightly chilled.

PREPARATION TIME
15 minutes

COOKING TIME
12 minutes

NUTRITIONAL VALUE PER SERVE	FAT 13.1 G	CARBOHYDRATE 18.7 G	PROTEIN 10.6 G

Lobster pineapple salad

INGREDIENTS

1 ripe pineapple with the top on
500 g (1 lb) cooked lobster meat
500 g (1 lb) cooked fish fillets
3 stalks celery, chopped
115 g (4 oz) blanched almonds,
  chopped
$^2/_3$ (170 ml, 5$^1/_2$ fl oz) cup mayonnaise
1 teaspoon curry powder
$^1/_2$ cup (125 ml, 4 fl oz) plain yoghurt
serves 6-8

1 Cut the pineapple lengthwise through the leaves and down to the base. Cut out the pineapple flesh, cut into chunks removing any core. Scrape inside of shell reserving any juice. Set shells aside for serving.

2 Cut the lobster meat into dice and break the fish fillets into bite-sized pieces. Combine lobster, reserved pineapple juice and fish pieces. Cover and refrigerate for 2 hours.

3 Mix the celery, almonds and pineapple chunks together. Add the lobster and fish pieces. Mix mayonnaise, curry powder and yoghurt together and carefully toss through the salad. Pile into the pineapple shells.

PREPARATION TIME
30 minutes, plus
2 hours refrigeration

NUTRITIONAL VALUE PER SERVE	FAT 7.3 G	CARBOHYDRATE 4.2 G	PROTEIN 10.6 G

Japanese marinated salmon, cucumber and daikon salad

INGREDIENTS

700 g (1 lb 7 oz) fillet salmon,
  centre cut
6 tablespoons mirin
3 tablespoons soy sauce
1 tablespoon grated fresh ginger
1 teaspoon sesame oil
1 continental cucumber, washed
1 teaspoon sea salt
1 tablespoon castor sugar
3 tablespoons rice vinegar
1 endive (curly chicory)
1 daikon (Japanese white radish),
  finely julienned
serves 6–8

PREPARATION TIME
30 minutes, plus
2 hours marinating

1 Using an extremely sharp knife, slice the salmon very thinly placing the knife at an angle. Place the slices neatly in a flat based dish.

2 Whisk together mirin, soy, ginger and sesame oil then remove 2 tablespoons and reserve. Pour the remainder over the sliced salmon and cover with plastic wrap. Place in the refrigerator to marinate for 2 hours.

3 Using a potato peeler or food slicer cut the cucumber into long, thin ribbons from each side avoiding the seeds. Break chicory into bite-sized pieces and in a large bowl toss together with cucumber and daikon. Mix together the sea salt, sugar and rice vinegar and toss through the salad.

4 Pile the endive salad into the centre of individual entrée plates or a large platter and arrange the marinated salmon around the edge. Drizzle reserved mirin over the salad.

NUTRITIONAL VALUE PER SERVE   FAT 3.4 G   CARBOHYDRATE 1.8 G   PROTEIN 8.8 G

Prawn and grape salad

INGREDIENTS

1 kg (2 lb) cooked prawns
1 cup (250 ml, 8 fl oz) sour cream
1 cup (250 g, 8 oz) mayonnaise
juice of 1 small lemon
¼ teaspoon tabasco sauce
2 cups white grapes, washed,
   dried and stems removed
2 tablespoons chopped fresh dill
2 tablespoons chopped fresh chives
freshly ground black pepper to taste
serves 4

PREPARATION TIME
10 minutes, plus
4 hours refrigeration

1 Shell and devein the prawns. Whisk the sour cream, mayonnaise, lemon juice and tabasco together.

2 Put prepared prawns into a serving bowl. Pour over dressing and toss gently. Add the grapes and toss again. Sprinkle on chopped dill and chives and pepper. Toss once more and refrigerate covered, for at least 4 hours.

| NUTRITIONAL VALUE PER SERVE | FAT **8.1** G | CARBOHYDRATE **5** G | PROTEIN **12.1** G |

Sweet potato and peanut salad

INGREDIENTS

2 kg (4 lb) sweet potato, peeled
6 tablespoons olive oil
20 cloves garlic, unpeeled
salt and pepper
1 Spanish onion, finely chopped
1–2 small red chillies, finely chopped
2 handfuls fresh herbs of
   your choice
2 tablespoons balsamic vinegar
320 g (11 oz) roasted peanuts
salt and freshly ground pepper
serves 10–12

1 Peel and cut the sweet potato into large chunks. Toss with 2 tablespoons of the olive oil and place in a large baking dish with the garlic cloves. Season to taste with salt and pepper and bake at 220°C (425°F, gas mark 7) for about 40 minutes or until the sweet potato is tender and golden around the edges. Remove from the oven.

2 Place cooked sweet potato on a platter, mix the spanish onion, chilli, fresh herbs together and sprinkle over the sweet potato.

3 Whisk the remaining 4 tablespoons olive oil with the salt and pepper and balsamic vinegar, drizzle over the sweet potato. Sprinkle the peanuts over and gently toss the salad. Serve immediately.

PREPARATION TIME
15 minutes

COOKING TIME
40 minutes

NUTRITIONAL VALUE PER SERVE   FAT **9.4** G   CARBOHYDRATE **12.2** G   PROTEIN **4.3** G

Thai rice salad

INGREDIENTS

3 tablespoons oil
1 tablespoon Thai curry paste
1 tablespoon brown sugar
2 tablespoons lemon juice
4 cups (740 g, 1½ lb) cooked
   long-grain rice
1 red capsicum (pepper), chopped
6 spring onions (green onions),
   chopped
440 g (14 oz) can pineapple pieces,
   drained
1 handful mint, chopped
salt
¼ teaspoon ground black pepper
serves 6

1 Heat 1 tablespoon of oil in a small frying pan, add curry paste and fry while stirring for 40 seconds. Remove from heat, add remaining oil, brown sugar, lemon juice and stir well to combine.

2 In a large bowl, place cooked rice and add curry mixture. Toss until mixed through. Add capsicum, onions, pineapple pieces, mint, salt and pepper. Toss well. Refrigerate until ready to serve.

PREPARATION TIME
10 minutes

COOKING TIME
3 minutes

NUTRITIONAL VALUE PER SERVE   FAT **4.5** G   CARBOHYDRATE **17.9** G   PROTEIN **1.7** G

Thai beef salad with chilli lime dressing

INGREDIENTS

500 g (1 lb) beef tenderloin (fillet)
in one piece
2 cloves garlic, crushed
3 tablespoons chopped
fresh coriander
2 tablespoons olive oil
1 tablespoon sweet chilli sauce
2 tablespoons lime juice
2 teaspoons Thai fish sauce
2 teaspoons soft light brown sugar
½ teaspoon ground cumin
250 g (8 oz) mixed salad leaves,
washed and crisped
3 tablespoons fresh mint leaves
3 spring onions (green onions),
diagonally sliced
1 red capsicum (pepper),
sliced for garnish
serves 4

1 Preheat oven to 220°C (425°F, gas mark 7). Trim off the silvery membrane and brush the fillet with oil. Place in a shallow tray and roast in oven for 25 minutes until medium rare. If using a meat thermometer, cook until it reaches 65°C to 70°C (135°F).

2 Remove from oven, cover with foil and rest for 20 minutes. Hold the end firmly with a strip of foil and using a sharp knife, slice very finely.

3 In a bowl, combine garlic, coriander, oil, chilli sauce, lime juice, fish sauce, sugar and cumin. Arrange salad leaves on a serving platter, drizzle with some of the dressing. Arrange the beef slices on top and pour over remaining dressing. Sprinkle with mint leaves, spring onions and capsicum strips.

PREPARATION TIME
20 minutes

COOKING TIME
25 minutes

NUTRITIONAL VALUE PER SERVE	FAT **8.5** G	CARBOHYDRATE **1.9** G	PROTEIN **14.7** G

Tropical prawn
and pawpaw salad

INGREDIENTS

salad
1 iceberg lettuce, washed and crisped
1 radicchio lettuce, washed
   and crisped
1 large avocado, cut into chunks
1 large grapefruit, segmented
1 pawpaw (papaya), deseeded
   and cut into chunks
24 medium-sized prawns,
   cooked and peeled

dressing
5 tablespoons white-wine vinegar
1 egg yolk, beaten
1 clove garlic, crushed
$\frac{1}{2}$ cup (125 ml, 4 fl oz) olive oil
1 tablespoon snipped fresh chives
salt
serves 4-6

PREPARATION TIME
15 minutes

1 In a bowl, whisk the vinegar, egg yolk, garlic, oil and chives, and salt to
taste until well-combined.

2 Mix the lettuces in a large bowl. Add just enough dressing to moisten
and toss until lightly coated. Pile in the centre of four plates.

3 Arrange the avocado, grapefruit, paw paw and prawns on and around
the lettuce. Drizzle with a little dressing and serve the remainder of
the dressing separately.

NUTRITIONAL VALUE PER SERVE	FAT 8.4 G	CARBOHYDRATE 1.3 G	PROTEIN 2.4 G

Glossary

Al dente: Italian term to describe pasta and rice that are cooked until tender but still firm to the bite.

Bake blind: to bake pastry cases without their fillings. Line the raw pastry case with greaseproof paper and fill with raw rice or dried beans to prevent collapsed sides and puffed base. Remove paper and fill 5 minutes before completion of cooking time.

Baste: to spoon hot cooking liquid over food at intervals during cooking to moisten and flavour it.

Beat: to make a mixture smooth with rapid and regular motions using a spatula, wire whisk or electric mixer; to make a mixture light and smooth by enclosing air.

Beurre manié: equal quantities of butter and flour mixed together to a smooth paste and stirred bit by bit into a soup, stew or sauce while on the heat to thicken. Stop adding when desired thickness results.

Bind: to add egg or a thick sauce to hold ingredients together when cooked.

Blanch: to plunge some foods into boiling water for less than a minute and immediately plunge into iced water. This is to brighten the colour of some vegetables; to remove skin from tomatoes and nuts.

Blend: to mix 2 or more ingredients thoroughly together; do not confuse with blending in an electric blender.

Boil: to cook in a liquid brought to boiling point and kept there.

Boiling point: when bubbles rise continually and break over the entire surface of the liquid, reaching a temperature of 100°C (212°F). In some cases food is held at this high temperature for a few seconds then heat is turned to low for slower cooking. See simmer.

Bouquet garni: a bundle of several herbs tied together with string for easy removal, placed into pots of stock, soups and stews for flavour. A few sprigs of fresh thyme, parsley and bay leaf are used. Can be purchased in sachet form for convenience.

Caramelise: to heat sugar in a heavy-based pan until it liquefies and develops a caramel colour. Vegetables such as blanched carrots and sautéed onions may be sprinkled with sugar and caramelised.

Chill: to place in the refrigerator or stir over ice until cold.

Clarify: to make a liquid clear by removing sediments and impurities. To melt fat and remove any sediment.

Coat: to dust or roll food items in flour to cover the surface before the food is cooked. Also, to coat in flour, egg and breadcrumbs.

Cool: to stand at room temperature until some or all heat is removed, e.g. cool a little, cool completely.

Cream: to make creamy and fluffy by working the mixture with the back of a wooden spoon, usually refers to creaming butter and sugar or margarine. May also be creamed with an electric mixer.

Croutons: small cubes of bread, toasted or fried, used as an addition to salads or as a garnish to soups and stews.

Crudite: raw vegetable sticks served with a dipping sauce.

Crumb: to coat foods in flour, egg and breadcrumbs to form a protective coating for foods which are fried. Also adds flavour, texture and enhances appearance.

Cube: to cut into small pieces with six even sides, e.g. cubes of meat.

Cut in: to combine fat and flour using 2 knives scissor fashion or with a pastry blender, to make pastry.

Deglaze: to dissolve dried out cooking juices left on the base and sides of a roasting dish or frying pan. Add a little water, wine or stock, scrape and stir over heat until dissolved. Resulting liquid is used to make a flavoursome gravy or added to a sauce or casserole.

Degrease: to skim fat from the surface of cooking liquids, e.g. stocks, soups, casseroles.

Dice: to cut into small cubes.

Dredge: to heavily coat with icing sugar, sugar, flour or cornflour.

Dressing: a mixture added to completed dishes to add moisture and flavour, e.g. salads, cooked vegetables.

Drizzle: to pour in a fine thread-like stream moving over a surface.

Egg wash: beaten egg with milk or water used to brush over pastry, bread dough or biscuits to give a sheen and golden brown colour.

Essence: a strong flavouring liquid, usually made by distillation. Only a few drops are needed to flavour.

Fillet: a piece of prime meat, fish or poultry which is boneless or has all bones removed.

Flake: to separate cooked fish into flakes, removing any bones and skin, using 2 forks.

Flame: to ignite warmed alcohol over food or to pour into a pan with food, ignite then serve.

Flute: to make decorative indentations around the pastry rim before baking.

Fold in: combining of a light, whisked or creamed mixture with other ingredients. Add a portion of the other ingredients at a time and mix using a gentle circular motion, over and under the mixture so that air will not be lost. Use a silver spoon or spatula.

Glaze: to brush or coat food with a liquid that will give the finished product a glossy appearance, and on baked products, a golden brown colour.

Grease: to rub the surface of a metal or heatproof dish with oil or fat, to prevent the food from sticking.

Herbed butter: softened butter mixed with finely chopped fresh herbs and re-chilled. Used to serve on grilled meats and fish.

Hors D'Oeuvre: small savoury foods served as an appetiser, popularly known today as 'finger food'.

Infuse: to steep foods in a liquid until the liquid absorbs their flavour.

Joint: to cut poultry and game into serving pieces by dividing at the joint.

Julienne: to cut some food, e.g. vegetables and processed meats into fine strips the length of matchsticks. Used for inclusion in salads or as a garnish to cooked dishes.

Knead: to work a yeast dough in a pressing, stretching and folding motion with the heel of the hand until smooth and elastic to develop the gluten strands. Non-yeast doughs should be lightly and quickly handled as gluten development is not desired.

Line: to cover the inside of a baking tin with paper for the easy removal of the cooked product from the baking tin.

Macerate: to stand fruit in a syrup, liqueur or spirit to give added flavour.

Marinade: a flavoured liquid, into which food is placed for some time to give it flavour and to tenderise. Marinades include an acid ingredient such as vinegar or wine, oil and seasonings.

Mask: to evenly cover cooked food portions with a sauce, mayonnaise or savoury jelly.

Pan-fry: to fry foods in a small amount of fat or oil, sufficient to coat the base of the pan.

Parboil: to boil until partially cooked. The food is then finished by some other method.

Pare: to peel the skin from vegetables and fruit. Peel is the popular term but pare is the name given to the knife used; paring knife.

Pith: the white lining between the rind and flesh of oranges, grapefruit and lemons.

Pit: to remove stones or seeds from olives, cherries, dates.

Pitted: the olives, cherries, dates etc. with the stone removed, e.g. purchase pitted dates.

Poach: to simmer gently in enough hot liquid to almost cover the food so shape will be retained.

Pound: to flatten meats with a meat mallet; to reduce to a paste or small particles with a mortar and pestle.

Simmer: to cook in liquid just below boiling point at about 96°C (205°F) with small bubbles rising gently to the surface.

Skim: to remove fat or froth from the surface of simmering food.

Stock: the liquid produced when meat, poultry, fish or vegetables have been simmered in water to extract the flavour. Used as a base for soups, sauces, casseroles etc. Convenience stock products are available.

Sweat: to cook sliced onions or vegetables, in a small amount of butter in a covered pan over low heat, to soften them and release flavour without colouring.

Conversions

Measurements differ from country to country, so it's important to understand what the differences are. This Measurements Guide gives you simple 'at-a-glance' information for using the recipes in this book, wherever you may be.

Cooking is not an exact science – minor variations in measurements won't make a difference to your cooking.

EQUIPMENT

There is a difference in the size of measuring cups used internationally, but the difference is minimal (only 2–3 teaspoons). We use the Australian standard metric measurements in our recipes:

1 teaspoon ....5 ml	1 tablespoon....20 ml
1/2 cup......125 ml	1 cup.....250 ml
4 cups...1 litre	

Measuring cups come in sets of one cup (250 ml), 1/2 cup (125 ml), 1/3 cup (80 ml) and 1/4 cup (60 ml). Use these for measuring liquids and certain dry ingredients.

Measuring spoons come in a set of four and should be used for measuring dry and liquid ingredients.

When using cup or spoon measures always make them level (unless the recipe indicates otherwise).

DRY VERSUS WET INGREDIENTS

While this system of measures is consistent for liquids, it's more difficult to quantify dry ingredients. For instance, one level cup equals: 200 g of brown sugar; 210 g of castor sugar; and 110 g of icing sugar.

When measuring dry ingredients such as flour, don't push the flour down or shake it into the cup. It is best just to spoon the flour in until it reaches the desired amount. When measuring liquids use a clear vessel indicating metric levels.

Always use medium eggs (55–60 g) when eggs are required in a recipe.

OVEN

Your oven should always be at the right temperature before placing the food in it to be cooked. Note that if your oven doesn't have a fan you may need to cook food for a little longer.

MICROWAVE

It is difficult to give an exact cooking time for microwave cooking. It is best to watch what you are cooking closely to monitor its progress.

STANDING TIME

Many foods continue to cook when you take them out of the oven or microwave. If a recipe states that the food needs to 'stand' after cooking, be sure not to overcook the dish.

CAN SIZES

The can sizes available in your supermarket or grocery store may not be the same as specified in the recipe. Don't worry if there is a small variation in size – it's unlikely to make a difference to the end result.

dry		liquids	
metric (grams)	imperial (ounces)	metric (millilitres)	imperial (fluid ounces)
		30 ml	1 fl oz
30 g	1 oz	60 ml	2 fl oz
60 g	2 oz	90 ml	3 fl oz
90 g	3 oz	100 ml	3 1/2 fl oz
100 g	3 1/2 oz	125 ml	4 fl oz
125 g	4 oz	150 ml	5 fl oz
150 g	5 oz	190 ml	6 fl oz
185 g	6 oz	250 ml	8 fl oz
200 g	7 oz	300 ml	10 fl oz
250 g	8 oz	500 ml	16 fl oz
280 g	9 oz	600 ml	20 fl oz (1 pint)*
315 g	10 oz	1000 ml (1 litre)	32 fl oz
330 g	11 oz		
370 g	12 oz		
400 g	13 oz		
440 g	14 oz		
470 g	15 oz		
500 g	16 oz (1 lb)		
750 g	24 oz (1 1/2 lb)		
1000 g (1 kg)	32 oz (2 lb)		*Note: an American pint is 16 fl oz.

cooking temperatures	°C (celsius)	°F (fahrenheit)	gas mark
very slow	120	250	1/2
slow	150	300	2
moderately slow	160	315	2–3
moderate	180	350	4
moderate hot	190	375	5
	200	400	6
hot	220	425	7
very hot	230	450	8
	240	475	9
	250	500	10

Index

Essential COOKING SERIES
COMPREHENSIVE, STEP BY STEP COOKING

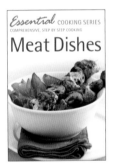

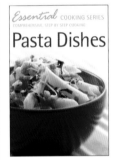

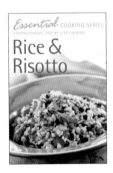

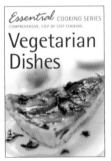

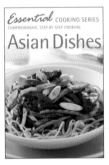